Contents

ACKNOWLEDGEMENTS

Illustrations are acknowledged as follows: Directors of the National Portrait Gallery, page 2; Radio Times Hulton Picture Library, pages 4, 19; Directors of the British Museum, page 7 (left); Trustees of the Watts Gallery, page 7 (right); Elsa M. Megson, pages 16 (top), 17 (both), 32; Cadbury Lamb, pages 20 (both), 21; Quentin Lloyd, Esq., page 35; Beatrix Farrand Collection, University of California, Berkeley, page 37 (both); Directors of the Tate Gallery and Miss Marguerite Steen, page 43.

Cover design by Richard Lewington, based on a photograph of Munstead Wood.

Printed in Great Britain by C. I. Thomas & Sons (Haverfordwest) Ltd, Press Buildings, Merlins Bridge, Haverfordwest.

Joseph Jekyll, Gertrude's grandfather, was a barrister and politician. He was a founder of the Athenaeum Club and a Fellow of the Royal Society of Arts.

Lifelines 37

Gertrude Jekyll

An illustrated life of Gertrude Jekyll

1843-1932

Betty Massingham

Shire Publications Ltd.

Gertrude Jekyll, a portrait by William Nicholson painted in 1920. Nicholson was a friend and neighbour of Edwin Lutyens, who persuaded Miss Jekyll to sit for the artist. Even so, the artist had to work in poor light for much of the time, for Miss Jekyll did not wish to waste the best part of the day away from her work.

Early life 1843-66

CHILDHOOD

Born on 29th November 1843, Gertrude Jekyll had an elder sister and four brothers. Her family can be traced back to the sixteenth century but one of her most distinguished forbears was her grandfather, Joseph Jekyll (1753-1837). A politician, well known for his ready wit, he was also a barrister and one of the founders of the Athenaeum Club and was elected a Fellow of the Royal Society of Arts. Her parents both studied various branches of the arts.

Two of her earliest recollections were a preference for almond sweets and making daisy chains in the garden of Berkeley Square. The key for the garden was kept at the recently opened Gunter's and the commissionaire who gave the children the key also gave them the sweets. When it was not hot enough to sit in the Berkeley Square garden they went for walks in Green Park, where the main attraction was the dandelions. And so, although a London child until she was nearly five years old, Gertrude Jekyll's first memories were country ones.

In 1848 her family moved from their Grafton Street home to Bramley House, about three miles south-west of Guildford. In a description written years later she speaks of 'biggish spaces, of garden and shrubbery and two ponds . . .' In one of the ponds there was a 'sort of enchanted land. It had some great poplars growing on it, and a tangle of undergrowth. Some of this came down and dipped into the water and here the moorhens built'.

There were few restrictions and her true contact with nature and with country people began. There was the carpenter, where she used to watch the planing of floor boards; the carrier who brought their parcels from Guildford station in a dogcart; the saddler; and the wharfinger who taught her to fish in the canal with a cast-net.

At about this time her governess gave her a copy of *Flowers of the*

5

Field, by the Rev. C. A. Johns. She wore one copy out completely and later on possessed two more, always keeping one close at hand for reference. Her background at home was intellectual and artistic. She was greatly interested in Greek art, drawing and painting, and music.

Her mother was a pupil of Mendelssohn, and musical evenings were an important part of the family life. Engrossed by the country, by music and painting, outside events hardly entered into her life at this time. She was now only just in her teens and the Crimean War may not have seemed very close at hand. She would probably have heard her parents mentioning the name of Florence Nightingale, but the general lack of speedy communications would mean that news penetrated slowly into this corner of West Surrey.

KENSINGTON SCHOOL OF ART

The year 1861 was an important one for Gertrude Jekyll. At seventeen she was an intelligent, cultured young woman, with a mind of her own, an interest in almost everyone and everything, and a sense of humour. She was also dauntless in the face of opposition to anything she particularly wanted to do.

She now took a characteristically intrepid step for a young lady at this time by enrolling as a student at the Kensington School of Art, where she studied for two years. The fact that her mother was an artist as well as a musician must have made the situation an easier one than for most daughters leaving school.

Although fashions and ideas were changing in the 1860s the world of painting, especially for young women, was still regarded with some suspicion. In 1853 Queen Victoria had been shown studies in the nude by Mulready and surprised everyone by wanting to buy one. She was expected to be shocked.

FOREIGN TRAVEL AND THE NEWTONS

Now there came the next event of importance in Gertrude Jekyll's life: 'When I was just grown up, though still in my late teens, I had the great advantage of going with friends (the Newtons) to the near East — the Greek islands, Constantinople, Smyrna, and Athens with several weeks in Rhodes.'

Charles Newton, the distinguished orientalist and excavator of Halicarnassus, was Keeper of the Greek and Roman Antiquities at the

(Left) Charles Newton, keeper of Greek and Roman Antiquities at the British Museum, a portrait by Henry Wyndham Phillips.
(Right) George Frederick Watts, a self-portrait.

British Museum. Mary Newton, herself an artist, was the daughter of Joseph Severn, the painter, friend and companion of Keats, and was closely linked with Ruskin. Her brother, Arthur Severn, was his life-long friend, and her husband was his contemporary at Oxford. Gertrude, who had been a fervent follower of Ruskin through the schoolroom, was now moving into his circle and was to become a close friend of the Newtons. Every connection seemed at this time to lead towards painting, and this journey with the Newtons must be recognised as a most important influence on the whole of Gertrude Jekyll's life and work.

At twenty-three, with a picture hung at Burlington House to her credit, Miss Jekyll spent much of her time in the National Gallery making copies of paintings by Turner and Watts, and she saw a great deal of the Newtons, going with them to the Academy, museums and art exhibitions. They were her dearest friends and must have influenced her considerably.

It was a great personal loss in her life when Mary Newton fell ill with a severe attack of measles and died at her home in Gower Street in 1866. It must have been gratifying, and some small consolation, that she was able to continue their work in Greece by illustrating the course of lectures given by Sir Charles Newton during the next year.

A woman of many talents

In 1866, with her cousin Georgina Duff Gordon, she visited Paris where she copied manuscripts at the Louvre and took singing lessons with Galvani. The spring of 1867 was spent in London attending Fiori's classes in Grosvenor Square and again making copies of Turner in the National Gallery. On 16th June she visited Mr Watts at Little Holland House where she copied his 'white oxen'. This was the beginning of a long friendship with the Watts family, who years later came to live near her home.

Early in 1868 she travelled on her first visit to Italy via the Riviera and Genoa and settled in Rome. This time she went with a fellow student, Susan Muir Mackenzie, who was described as 'brilliant, musical and artistic', and who modelled the portrait of Esther for Millais. It was in Rome that Gertrude Jekyll became engrossed in the study of carving and gilding under the tuition of a local craftsman. 'An Italian who has "carver and gilder" over his shop really does carve and gild. The kindly *padrone* put me through a piece of work from beginning to end. First, the carving of the frame, then the successive coats of size and whitening, and the use of certain steel tools . . .' The process ended with 'the floating on of the gold leaf'.

A CHANGE OF HOME

On her return to England in April 1868 she found herself faced with a move of the family home from Bramley to Wargrave, in Berkshire.

There may have been disadvantages in moving from Bramley, but at least the journey to London was no more difficult than it had been, and so her art studies could continue. There were still stimulating meetings with Ruskin and with G. F. Watts and there is a note of an appointment to see William Morris, in March 1869. It was also in March of this year that Ruskin was lecturing on Greek mythology at University College. These lectures were the basis of *The Queen of the Air,* published later in the year, and in the preface Ruskin especially mentions his friendship with Sir Charles Newton, who probably first fired him with interest in this subject.

Miss Jekyll was fortunate in her friends. First there had been the Newtons, who had introduced her to the Ruskin circle. The ideas of Ruskin and William Morris were being published, eagerly read and discussed. *A Joy for Ever and its Price in the Market* contained the Ruskin lectures dealing with working conditions which had been delivered in Manchester in 1857, and Ruskin was discussing housing with Octavia Hill in 1867. Then there were the Blumenthals; at their home at 43 Hyde Park Gate they frequently held musical evenings and it was at one of these occasions that she met Brabazon, the water-colourist. Having become a friend of Brabazon, she met through him Barbara Leigh Smith (Barbara Bodichon), who apart from being one of the founders of Girton, was also an artist, numbering among her friends Rossetti, Corot and Daubigny, and had painted enough to make a thousand pounds from the sale of her work to give towards the foundation of this first college for women.

Brabazon was the most important of these new friends owing to his influence as a painter. It was from him that Miss Jekyll learnt her lessons in colour. He 'carried on the tradition of Turner's later and more abstract water-colours . . .' 'Light and colour became the essence, the reason of his pictures . .'

The Duke of Westminster, a visitor at Morpeth Terrace (the home of Miss Jekyll's brother) and a fellow guest at the Blumenthals' musical parties, called Gertrude Jekyll in for advice on the furnishings at Eaton Hall, after the extensive alterations carried out there in 1870. These were on a grand scale. The work of craftsmen and artists from various parts of the Continent and from this country was brought together: 'the drawing room is elaborately decorated and has silk embroidered panels, designed by Miss Jekyll, and executed by the Royal School of Art Needlework at South Kensington.' The work for Eaton Hall went on throughout the winter and in 1875 the Duke of Westminster was writing to ask her to undertake the responsibility for the whole of the furnishing and to give her advice generally.

RETURN TO WEST SURREY

Soon there was to be a move once more of the family home — this time from Berkshire back to Miss Jekyll's beloved West Surrey. The move, occasioned by the death of her father in 1876, took place within a year. The family had by this time been reduced to three owing to the marriages of the older brothers and her sister Carry, and their Wargrave house was now too big for them.

The selection of Munstead House, near Godalming, was made for various reasons, one being that it was reasonably near to Bramley House, their old home, and another that it was accessible to London from Godalming station.

Miss Jekyll's friendship with William Robinson was developing, perhaps because of the articles she had written for his journal *The Garden*. In 1880 Robinson visited the Munstead garden, taking with him Dean Hole, who had organised the first Rose Show eleven years before. Her near neighbour was now G. F. Wilson, whose property close to Cobham has since become well-known as the Wisley Royal Horticultural Society's gardens.

In 1881 Miss Jekyll was asked to judge at the Botanic Show — precursor of the now famous Chelsea Flower Show.

SEPARATE ESTABLISHMENTS

Mrs Jekyll, who was now well over seventy, began to find the constant stream of visitors to the house rather tiring. It was decided that separate establishments should be occupied by mother and daughter, to allow for greater freedom for the one and greater quiet for the other. A strip of land, about fifteen acres, adjoining Munstead on the northern side was purchased, and the foundations of Miss Jekyll's own garden were laid although the house was not yet built.

1883 found her once more visiting friends abroad — Capri, Naples, Rome, Florence, Alassio and Genoa in Italy — and making a special pilgrimage to visit the cathedrals of Sens and Amiens on the way back through France.

The summer of 1884 seems to have been spent at Munstead and in the autumn a holiday was taken exploring the Severn district.

In 1885 Gertrude Jekyll took up a new interest, the art of photography, then in its infancy. As with all her other interests this was done thoroughly, sinks and dark rooms being fitted up for experiments, and farm buildings, lanes and trees were tried out as suitable subjects. Her enthusiasm led her to get up at 4 o'clock in the early morning so that certain shots might be photographed with success.

A MEETING OF IMPORTANCE

One afternoon in 1889 Miss Jekyll visited her friend and neighbour, Mr Harry Mangles of Littleworth, who was one of the pioneers of rhododendron growing. On this occasion there was another guest who was to prove of special interest, a young man aged twenty working nearby on his first architectural commission. Edwin Lutyens describes

11

the meeting over the teacups, 'the silver kettle and the conversation reflecting rhododendrons'.

Miss Jekyll must have liked him instantly as she invited him to go to tea with her at Munstead on the following Saturday. She was reserved and quiet when he first met her and during the course of the tea-party did not speak to him at all. But outside, as she was leaving, 'with one foot on the step of her pony-cart and reins in hand', the invitation was given and accepted.

This meeting and the friendship that followed were to shape her life in the crisis which was coming very close. The summer months were still taken up with painting and working in the new garden, visits to friends — Madame Bodichon, Hercules Brabazon, the Blumenthals — the winter months with dark-room work, silver-work and wood carving.

In December of this year she wrote the following letter to Brabazon which mentions and in a way sums up most of her activities at this time.

Dec. 13th/89.   Munstead, Godalming.

Dear Mr Brabazon, We are very glad to have news of you after a rather long interval. . . . It is just that with our dear Madame Bodichon — an enduring joy to have known her! It is always good news to hear of her being in any degree well and able to enjoy anything, as she really does in spite of her crippled state. I hope to be with her again in March and to find her no worse again.

I am very sorry that Mr Sargent is out of the way, as a Brabazon Exhibition is a thing much to be desired, but I shall hope to hear that Goupil 'means business'.

We are all very well; my mother, as usual, younger than anybody. I have been doing some vigorous landscape gardening for home and friends — doing living pictures with land and trees and flowers!

I suppose you know the Blumenthals are at Hyde Park Gate — a month earlier than usual. I hope to be with them for a few days early in January.

Yours very truly,
Gertrude Jekyll.

To all appearances the same life was going on in much the same pattern, and there was little sign of the approaching disaster round the corner.

A change of direction

FAILING EYESIGHT

For many years Miss Jekyll's eyes had troubled her. She must have been physically strong, as well as mentally alert, to fit in so much work during these years, but some of the finer details, especially the embroidery and the painting, were proving a strain on her eyes. She was short-sighted as a girl and a drawing by Mary Newton on the Greek trip shows her wearing glasses.

Work went on, but it is believed that she suffered a good deal of pain as well as inconvenience. In the summer of 1891 she was prevailed upon to consult the famous eye specialist Pagenstecher of Wiesbaden. The result may have seemed disastrous at the time, although in later life she acknowledged a certain debt to the myopia which at that moment crippled most of her hopes. Nearly all her work was discouraged if not forbidden, and in particular the two subjects she loved most, embroidery and painting. The oculist professed to be able only to arrest the condition but held out no hope of a cure.

In an article written many years later she refers to the incident with these words: 'When I was young I was hoping to be a painter, but to my lifelong regret, I was obliged to abandon all hope of this, after a certain amount of art school work, on account of extreme and always progressive myopia.'

She was nearly fifty years of age. Instead of marrying and bringing up a family she had concentrated her energies chiefly on painting, and afterwards on arts of all kinds. She had never wasted an opportunity of learning, from the most humble job in building construction to the use of colour on a canvas. Her value of time was such that she could have filled up every moment that was given to her with the industry of her talents. We know from her religious belief, which shines through her writing, that she would not be defeated by her failing eyesight and to combat it she had trained herself to be discriminating in what she observed.

13

NEW INTERESTS

A quantity of expensive and rare plants in a garden, with long Latin names written across their labels, would not have impressed Miss Jekyll even though she was familiar with the names herself. Affectation in any form was outside her province and she had no patience with it. The best illustration of this is her advice given freely and the trouble taken over a factory boy in Rochdale who wanted help with the planting of his window-box.

The boy had advertised in a mechanical paper for help in planting a window-box. Miss Jekyll wrote years later: 'he knew nothing — would somebody help him with advice? So advice was sent and the box prepared. If I remember rightly the size was three feet by ten inches. A little later the post brought him plants of mossy and silvery saxifrages, and a few small bulbs. Even some stones were sent, for it was to be a rock-garden, and there were to be two hills of different heights with rocky tops, and a longish valley with a sunny and shady side.'

Gardening did not require the very close scrutiny necessary for painting and embroidery and would not be such a strain on her eyes. It was to the circle of William Robinson and the Rev. Reynolds Hole, Mr Harry Mangles of Littleworth and Mr G. F. Wilson of Wisley, the Rev. Wolley Dod, Canon Ellacombe and Mr Edward Woodall that she was now able to turn. She came with a background of knowledge, interest and love for this subject which had developed alongside her other activities.

A NEW PARTNERSHIP

Perhaps the greatest compensation of all was to come through her friendship with the young Ned Lutyens. Sometimes they went round the lanes in the pony-cart discussing farm buildings and barns and varieties of materials and their uses. This was a new partnership, beginning at a crucial moment for both, which was to last for over forty years. To Miss Jekyll, nearly fifty, at a turning point when her greatest talent and interest was denied her, the enthusiasm and youth of Ned Lutyens must have provided exactly the right counterpart. She would never have had patience with the second-rate and must have recognised in Lutyens the possibilities of genius. Perhaps it was the greatest benefit that happened to either of them. It certainly produced something of lasting value to the English way of life.

In 1894 beginnings were made for Miss Jekyll's permanent home. First, 'the hut' was designed and built and of course discussed with Lutyens. This was to provide a temporary roof until he could have the

Photography was one of Gertrude Jekyll's many interests and she photographed this group at Munstead, including her brother Herbert's daughters Barbara and Pamela, Leonard Borwick, Hercules Brabazon and Miss Muir Mackenzie.

(Right) A modern photograph of the south side of the garden door at Munstead Wood, with clematis and choisya.

(Below) The overhanging part of the gallery at Munstead Wood, as it was. This unusual feature was incorporated by Lutyens because of Miss Jekyll's objection to narrow passages. She loved to walk along this gallery and chose to have her bedroom at one end of it.

(Above) Munstead Wood, the house near Godalming, Surrey, built by Edwin Lutyens for Miss Jekyll. She moved into her new home in October 1897.

(Right) In 'Home and Garden' Miss Jekyll wrote of Munstead Wood that 'one of the wishes I expressed to the architect was that I should like a little of the feeling of a convent.'

main house ready for her and then it was to act as an overflow for the workshop and gardening paraphernalia. 'The hut' was ready for occupation in November 1894, and she was a stage nearer to the realisation of the house Lutyens was to build, the plans for which she had been turning over in her mind for some years.

In July of the next year Mrs Jekyll died, after a week's illness, at the age of eighty-two. Munstead House was left to Herbert Jekyll with his family of three children, and there was every reason now for the hurrying on of a permanent home for his unmarried sister, so that she might be able to enjoy her Munstead garden from the windows of her own house. There was probably never before or since a happier collaboration between owner and architect than while the building of Munstead Wood was going forward. They both had the same feeling for the use of the right materials and they both felt the importance of an honest solidity and the inclusion of regional characteristics.

MUNSTEAD WOOD

In October 1897 Miss Jekyll moved from 'the hut' into Munstead Wood. The day before the move she received the award of the Victoria Medal of Honour from the Royal Horticultural Society. Her garden, already of some years' standing, was well-known in the horticultural world and visited by gardening enthusiasts from many parts of the country. Her relationship with Lutyens was expanding and it is interesting to reflect on how much they were each responsible for the success of a collaboration which produced such a contribution to the English way of life as 'a Lutyens house with a Jekyll garden'.

His son wrote of them: 'Much has he owed to her companionship and encouragement; much to her great knowledge of rural tradition . . . Whilst Miss Jekyll elaborated, with an infallibility of taste and sensitive craftsmanship, the growing feeling for natural and picturesque planting . . . she found in Father the ideal interpreter who eventually exalted her limited conception on to the plane of creative formal design.'

Inside the house there were many interesting features. The casement windows did not allow for too much light; this was done on purpose to save Miss Jekyll's eyes from the glare. The gallery was an important feature not only of this house, but one introduced by Lutyens into some of his other plans on account of its success here. It originated because Miss Jekyll stipulated against narrow passages and Lutyens found himself faced with one at the top of the staircase. By widening this into an overhanging gallery the width was achieved, while providing a

18

Sir Edwin Lutyens (1869-1944), the architect, first met Gertrude Jekyll at a tea-party in 1889. A fruitful partnership developed; a Lutyens house with a Jekyll garden became a part of the English way of life.

19

Hestercombe House, near Taunton, Somerset, has been said to mark the peak of the collaboration between Lutyens and Gertrude Jekyll. Now occupied by the Somerset County Fire Service, the gardens are undergoing careful restoration. Above is the orangery designed by Lutyens and, left, the pergola walk.

A lily-pond at Hestercombe. Miss Jekyll had a great feeling for the correct materials to use.

sheltered place to sit beneath out in the courtyard. Miss Jekyll so loved to walk through this gallery that she specially chose her bedroom to be at the further end of it. The use of a similar gallery in later plans by Lutyens gave a character of stability, spaciousness and clear outline to his work which helped to counteract some of the fussiness for which he was sometimes criticised. Notable examples are at Deanery Garden and at Lindisfarne.

Other requests made by Miss Jekyll to the architect included many cupboards with glass doors useful to a 'person of accumulative proclivity', as she described herself. Also she wanted a small house with spacious rooms — she would have 'nothing poky or screwy or ill lighted'.

EDWIN LUTYENS

By now Lutyens was a name in the architectural world. The addition to Crooksbury for the Chapmans (1899), Orchards, near Godalming, for Lady Chance (1898-9), Deanery Garden, Sonning, for E. H. Hudson (1899), Little Thakeham, Sussex (1902), Marsh Court, Stockbridge, Hampshire (1901) — all these were enlarging his reputation, and the basis and foundation of it all was the house built for Miss Jekyll at Munstead.

In 1904 Marsh Court and Thakeham were finished or nearing completion. Country Life Offices were commissioned and the renovation at Lindisfarne was on its way. New Place, Shedfield, was undertaken in 1905 and before New Place was finished he started work on Hestercombe.

Of the Hestercombe gardens Mr Hussey wrote: '(they) represent the peak of the collaboration with Miss Jekyll, and his first application of her genius to classical garden design on a grand scale.' In her book *Garden Ornament* which she wrote years later with Christopher Hussey, she describes the terrace and the steps leading down to the parterre where she had designed flower-beds bordered with bergenia. An example of her attention to detail, even in such a vast undertaking as this, is shown by the border of stone laid between the edges of the bergenia and the grass paths, in order to protect the plants and to make the mowing easier.

The orangery at Hestercombe is a splendid example of the best of Lutyens and the steps are of the same design as some of those at Deanery Garden, Sonning, and at Great Dixter.

Books and articles

HER FIRST BOOKS

Her writings were now becoming known. She had contributed to William Robinson's magazine *The Garden* for some time. The *National Review* published a short article on house decoration, and the *Edinburgh Review* a longer one on garden craft from ancient times until the nineteenth century. She was also writing periodical notes for the *Guardian* at irregular intervals as a guide for amateurs. These notes were collected together and in April 1898 an agreement with Messrs Longmans was reached for their publication in book form. The illustrations were to be taken from her own store of photographs.

The Longmans publication came out in 1899. It was called *Wood and Garden* — 'notes and thoughts, practical and critical, of a working amateur, with 71 illustrations from photographs by the author'. It ran into at least six editions in the first year and was so successful that the publishers urged her to follow it up with further notes on the garden and also on the house. These were published in 1900 under the title of *Home and Garden*.

The first of these two books contains the essence of Miss Jekyll's writing. She put all her heart and knowledge into it, all her experience from her travels abroad and her affection for grey-leaved plants. It is full of poetry in the writing and plain common sense in the information.

Apart from the monthly notes of what to do in the garden, flowering times of plants and similar information, there are chapters devoted to special subjects, and the book included some of her ideas on colour about which she later wrote a complete book. There is an encouraging chapter headed 'Beginning and Learning', showing an unusual understanding of the problems of beginners, the frustrations and the disappointments, and a consoling chapter on 'Large and Small Gardens' showing her interest and affection for a well-planned small

*A photograph of a woodland lane from 'Home and Garden'. Miss Jekyll wrote:
'. . . indeed an unmade woodland track is the nearest thing to a road-poem that
anything of the kind can show.'*

garden. 'I think that a garden should never be large enough to be tiring, that if a large space has to be dealt with, a great part had better be laid out in wood . . . I do not envy the owners of very large gardens.'

The chapter on 'The Scents of the Garden' refers especially to her much-loved grey-foliage plants. They recalled for her the travels to the Greek islands when she must have seen clumps of acanthus by the roadside, hedges of myrtle and rosemary, oleanders growing like willows and grassy banks crowned by the tall spikes of yuccas.

Miss Jekyll's religious belief comes into these books in her appreciation of beauty and the miracle of the seasons. 'There is always in February some one day, at least, when one smells the yet distant, but surely coming, summer. Perhaps it is a warm mossy scent . . . or it may be in some woodland opening, where the sun has coaxed out the pungent smell of the trailing ground ivy, whose blue flowers will soon appear, but the day always comes, and with it the glad certainty that summer is nearing, and the good things promised will never fail' (*Wood and Garden*).

A PROLIFIC WRITER

Then followed years of large literary output — almost a book a year — and of successful collaboration with Lutyens.

In 1901 *Lilies for English Gardens* (published by Country Life) made its appearance with the sub-title 'A Guide for Amateurs'. It was the result of a series of queries sent out to thirty known lily growers by the editors of *The Garden*. At the time, Miss Jekyll was co-editor with E. T. Cook. In the preface she remarks that many less-known lilies have been omitted. 'They concern the botanist, whose business it is to know and to classify everything; they scarcely concern the gardener whose interest it is to know what lilies will best grace his garden.'

Then came *Wall and Water Gardens,* also published in 1901. This is one of the most attractive of all her books, being written from the point of view that — as she explains to children — 'nothing is so delightful as playing with water'. A great deal of her philosophy is in this book, and there is poetry in the writing of it, too. Under the chapter heading 'When to Let Well Alone' she describes a certain wild forest pool. 'Here is a glimpse of quite natural beauty; pure nature untouched. Being in itself beautiful, and speaking direct to our minds of the poetry of the woodland, it would be an ill deed to mar its perfection by any meddlesome gardening. The most one could do in such a place, where deer may come down to drink and the dragonfly flash in the broken midsummer light, would be to plant in the upper ground some native wild flower that would be in harmony with the place but that may happen to be absent, such as wood sorrel or wood anemone.'

Roses for English Gardens was published in 1902 also by Country Life. The book was written in conjunction with Mr Edward Mawley, and divided into two parts, one part written by each author. Miss Jekyll's contribution, rather more than half the book, is entitled 'Old and New Roses and Their Beautiful Use in Gardens'. Mr Mawley deals with the more practical side of 'pruning, planting and propagating'.

The next literary venture was something of a rather different character. Away, this time, from roses, lilies, Munstead Wood, rock gardens and water gardens, and back to the memories of her childhood — the book is called *Old West Surrey*, published in 1904 by Longmans. This was enlarged and republished in 1925 by Batsford under the title of *Old English Household Life*.

The knowledge that Gertrude Jekyll had acquired from going in and out of cottages and cottage gardens, from driving down the lanes in her pony-cart, and from her knowledge of the cottages themselves, was quite prodigious. She knew about their customs and their means of living, and it is clear from her writing that she was an authority on all kinds of paving (ripple-marked stone, and iron-stone pitching), wells, bacon-lofts, gates, kitchen fireplaces, clocks, granaries, dairies, straw-plaiting, samplers, patchwork, candlesticks, thatching, inn signs, churchyards and tombstones, and the speech, manners and customs of the village people. She was also especially interested in bridges.

LINDISFARNE CASTLE

Another excitement at this time was when Edward Hudson acquired the ruins of Lindisfarne and asked Lutyens to restore the castle. This work went on during 1903-4, and was one of his best restorations. The atmosphere is welcoming, with a feeling of solidity but also of comfort. The wooden doors have large, heavy latches and the gallery — in the style of the Munstead gallery — is an important feature. It is all excellent in workmanship and in design. The garden planting was in Miss Jekyll's charge — and she herself visited the castle a year or two later.

A drawing by Lutyens of Gertrude Jekyll, made about 1896.

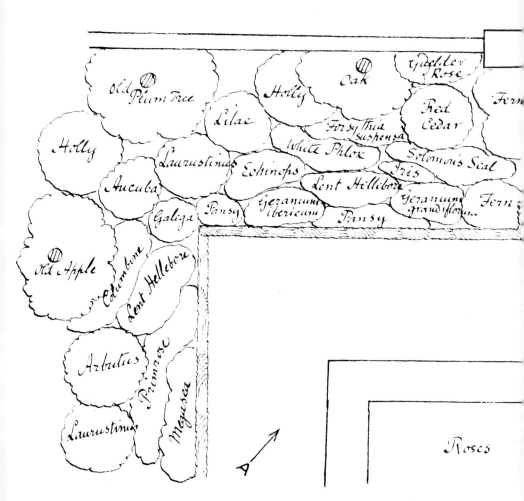

(Above) Miss Jekyll's planting plan for part of the garden at Millmead, Bramley, where she worked with Lutyens. Part of the area, viewed from point A on the plan, is seen in the photograph (right). The summerhouse is at the top right-hand part of the plan. The plan and photograph are from 'Gardens for Small Country Houses' by Miss Jekyll and Lawrence Weaver.

Other collaborations with Lutyens included: Folly Farm, Sulhamstead, Berkshire; Hestercombe, Somerset; and — perhaps one of the most exciting for them both — Millmead, Bramley — a small house with a small garden.

In 1906 came the death of H. B. Brabazon — a sad loss to her — and in 1907 a further publication — *Flower Decoration in the House.*

CHILDREN AND GARDENS

Two more books were published in 1908, one of them suggested by Edwin Lutyens. He felt that his family should be brought up from an early age in the gardening faith, and it seemed sensible that a reliable and interesting guide to gardening for children should be written. The result was *Children and Gardens* by Gertrude Jekyll.

A photograph from 'Children and Gardens' published in 1908. Miss Jekyll wrote this book at the suggestion of Lutyens who sensed the need for an interesting gardening guide for children.

Miss Jekyll's book for children would have been of little use, however technically accurate, if it had not been written in the language that children would understand and appreciate. Her capacity for entering into the world of a child was one of her greatest accomplishments. There are constant references throughout the book to humour, adventure and magic, and descriptions of some of her cats which were her constant companions.

COLOUR IN THE FLOWER GARDEN

The days spent as an art student and the painting accomplished later, until her eyes troubled her too greatly, now bore fruit in the other book which she published in 1908 — *Colour in the Flower Garden,* (subsequent editions entitled *Colour Schemes for the Flower Garden*). This book, as far as it is possible to judge at this distance of time, is her great contribution to English gardening. Her ideas on colour stand in a class apart.

In this book the essence of her artistic training is collected together and here she is first an artist and then a gardener. One of her most general ideas about the use of colour is that flowers which bloom at the same time should be arranged wherever possible close to each other. It is far better to have a clump of colour at one time of the year and then a space of green to follow, than to have bits of colour dotted about so that there is always something in flower in a particular bed or border of the garden.

Speaking again of the impossibility of continuous colour everywhere in the garden, she says '. . . it is even undesirable to have a garden in blossom all over, and groups of flower-beauty are all the more enjoyable for being more or less isolated, by stretches of intervening greenery.'

Probably her biggest contribution to the study of colour is that she has established that no colour stands alone and that it can only have real value if it is thought of in relation to the colours close beside it.

Orchards, near Godalming, was built in 1898-9 by Edwin Lutyens for Lady Chance. This commission, like many others, arose as a result of the architect's work with Miss Jekyll at Munstead Wood.

Cottage gardens

This was a time in English history when the cottage gardens were keeping the flag flying. In some of the estates and the larger gardens there was little imagination, only a good deal of ornamental bedding-out. The shape of the flower-bed was described as being more important than what went into it. Some of the precious flowers we love and treasure today were only to be found in cottage gardens, having been turned out in many cases in favour of half-hardy plants cosseted through the winter in Sir Joseph Paxton's greenhouses.

The cottage gardens, however, were untouched by this epidemic of bedding-out. William Cobbett (earlier in the century) writes ecstatically of them in his *Rural Rides:* '. . . and you see here, as in Kent, Surrey, Sussex and Hampshire, and indeed in almost every part of England, that most interesting of all objects, that which is such an honour to England, and that which distinguishes it from all the rest of the world, namely, those neatly kept and productive little gardens round the labourers' houses, which are seldom unornamented with more or less of flowers.'

LEARNING FROM COTTAGE GARDENS

Throughout her writings Gertrude Jekyll acknowledges not only her love for but also her debt to cottage gardens. In *Home and Garden* she expresses gratitude for small hints or useful ideas to be found there: 'It may be some two plants growing beautifully together by some happy chance, or a pretty mixed tangle of creepers, or something that one always thought must have a south wall doing better on an east one.' Then again, 'I have also learnt from cottage gardens how pretty are some of the old roses grown as standards . . . I have taken the hint, and have now some big round-headed standards, the heads a yard through, of the lovely Celeste and of Madame Plantier . . .' And, in *Colour Schemes for the Flower Garden,* 'I remember another cottage that had a porch covered with the golden balls of *Kerria japonica,* and China roses reaching up the greater part of the low walls of half timber and plastering . . .' There is another example of a wall plant introduced into her own garden on this account. 'In remembrance of the cottage example lately quoted there is *Pyrus japonica* under the long sitting-room window.'

One of Miss Jekyll's favourite plants was a yucca, and it was from a cottage garden that she had learnt a valuable secret for helping it through the winter. 'I found it in a cottage garden, where I learnt a useful lesson in protecting plants, namely, the use of thickly cut peaty sods. The goodwife had noticed that the peaty ground of the adjoining common, covered with heath and gorse and mossy grass, resisted frost much better than the garden or meadow, and it had been her practice for many years to get some thick dry sods with the heath left on and to pack them close round to protect tender plants.' This treatment applied particularly to half-hardy fuchsias and *Yucca filamentosa.*

Miss Jekyll was a gardening genius largely because she was alert and interested and ready to learn. 'But eye and brain must be alert to receive the impression and studious to store it.' And she went to the cottage gardens for much of her knowledge, because she felt that 'they have a simple and tender charm that one may look for in vain in gardens of greater pretension. And the old garden flowers seem to know that there they are seen at their best; for where else can one see such wallflowers, or double daisies, or white rose bushes; such clustering masses of perennial peas, or such well-kept flowery edgings of pink, or thrift, or London pride?' (*Home and Garden*).

USE OF MATERIALS

But it was not only the plants in the cottage gardens that she noticed on her drives with Lutyens. He must have learnt from her about the setting of a chimney, the different uses and patterns of tiles, the right proportions of windows and doorways — all matters essential to his work. As Robert Lutyens wrote: 'The influence of this wise, eccentric and cultivated woman on her generation in general, and on my father in particular, has been on the whole insufficiently acknowledged.' Mr Harold Falkner, himself an architect and her contemporary, was aware of this influence: 'Miss Jekyll had . . . a knowledge', he wrote in a letter to me some years ago, 'of the very finest building practices which she

The circular steps, designed by Lutyens in 1912, at Great Dixter, Northiam, in East Sussex.

transferred to Lutyens, and that "sense of material" made him different from all other architects of his time.'

In *Wall and Water Gardens* Miss Jekyll summed up the relationship of architect and gardener: 'for the best building and planting . . the architect and the gardener must have *some* knowledge of each other's business, and each must regard with feelings of kindly reverence the unknown domains of the other's higher knowledge.'

Sometimes a restoration can be more difficult to effect successfully than an original design. Lindisfarne Castle and Great Dixter are examples of Lutyens's application of the lessons learnt from his mentor.

MISS JEKYLL'S GARDEN PLANS

But perhaps it should be mentioned that Lutyens was not always the architect with whom Miss Jekyll worked. The Beatrix Farrand Collection of her garden plans at the University of California, Berkeley, shows not only the interesting pattern of her work and how it developed along certain lines as she grew older and more blind, but also that her ideas were much sought after throughout this country and sometimes in America. Often this involved working with other architects or firms of surveyors. Amongst these were Oliver Hill, Forbes and Tate, Percy

35

Adams, H. Baillie-Scott, Ernest Willmott and Sir R. Lorimer. But these are only some of the names which appear on certain of the plans during the years from about 1905 until just before she died in 1932. One of the last plans which she drew for a client was done in December 1931, when she had just passed her eighty-eighth birthday, and on this occasion she was working with the surveyors Usher and Anthony of Bedford.

The plans show, among other things, her regard for what is right in a certain position. She was known for her ideas on natural gardening but if a formal bedding-out area seemed appropriate and was desired by the owner she would happily co-operate. As she writes in *Wall and Water Gardens* (Country Life—5th edition 1913): 'For the formal garden of the best type I can picture to myself endless possibilities both of beauty and delight. . .' The idea that she was *only* interested in natural garden design appears from these plans to be erroneous. During the last fifteen to twenty years of her life she always made it clear that she was unable to travel to visit prospective gardens, however much she was tempted by the owner's promises of having easy transport arranged for her. 'It will only take you an hour to drive over, Miss Jekyll, and we will have you home before sunset' was the kind of persuasive argument produced on more than one occasion. However, she was firm in her refusal, but always asked for three guides to help in her designs. One of these was a surveyor's plan. She explained that this was essential at all times, even in the earlier days when she had been able to travel and see the garden herself. Then she always wanted to know if the owner had any favourite ideas or flowers or shrubs or tree planting, or perhaps a water garden, a rock garden, a wild garden, an orchard or a rose garden. Lastly she asked if there were any good opportunities for vistas, and if so, at what distance, and in which compass direction did they lie.

She herself loved designing and planting a rose garden, and gives in these plans many various collections of roses which she recommends for planting from her own personal experience. One of her favourites, amongst the climbing roses, was always Madame Alfred Carriére, and another was the deeply flushed pink Blairrii No. 2. She especially loved the Garland rose, and trained it into a suitable tree such as a catalpa, and amongst most lists appears the thornless bright pink of Zepherine Drouhin.

Plans drawn by Miss Jekyll for gardens at Barrington Court, Somerset: (above) 'garden C'; (below) the herb garden. These are amongst the Beatrix Farrand Collection of her garden plans at the University of California, Berkeley.

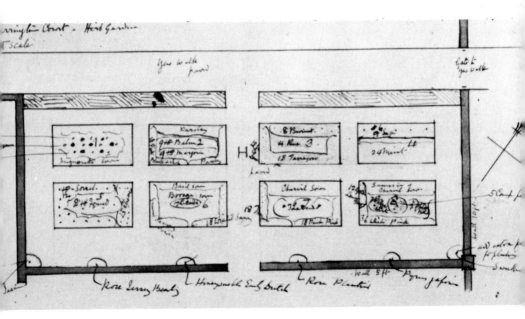

Two of Miss Jekyll's favourite plants, honeysuckle (above), beloved for its scent, and (left) lady's mantle, whose beautiful foliage she greatly admired.

Scent in the garden

Again and again in her writing, Miss Jekyll refers to the importance of the smell of a flower: 'One expects every rose to be fragrant . . .'; and 'The sweet scents of a garden are by no means the least of its many delights.' Apart from the enjoyment and the love of a scented garden, Miss Jekyll maintains that to recognise the smell of a flower is to get to know it. Writing especially for children, in *Children and Gardens,* she says: 'one finds out a great deal about flowers and plants by smelling them, and it is one of the most important ways of getting to know them.'

MISS JEKYLL'S FAVOURITES

To consider all the flowers and plants which Miss Jekyll mentions in connexion with sweet scent would be impossible, but here are a few of her favourites:

Primrose. 'It must have been at about seven years of age that I first learnt to know and love a primrose copse. Since then more than half a century has passed, and yet each spring, when I wander into the primrose wood and see the pale yellow blooms, and smell their sweetest of scents, . . . for a moment I am seven years old again and wandering in the fragrant wood . . .' (*A Gardener's Testament*). '. . . the first scent of the year's first primrose is no small pleasure' (*Wood and Garden*).

Wild honeysuckle. 'It throws out its crowns and garlands of sweetest scent' (*A Gardener's Testament*).

Mignonette. 'For mignonette is and always should be a plant of modest colouring and sweetest scent; both these qualities belong to the older kind . . .' (*Wood and Garden*).

Miss Jekyll writes of 'the sweetness of a sun-baked bank of wallflower' and 'the sweet-scented leafing of sweet-briar.'

Apple-blossom, small pansies, myrtle and the cabbage rose, a twig of bay, a tuft of thyme or a sprig of rosemary — all are mentioned, with many others. Pinks and carnations are an obvious selection, also lily of the valley, gardenia and jasmine. She mentions particularly the smell of dying strawberry leaves.

Then there are the night scents — among others, the evening primrose, tobacco-plants and night-scented stock. Miss Jekyll remarks on the impossibility of getting these scents at any other time: 'I have tried hard in daytime to get a whiff of the night sweetness of *Nicotiana affinis,* but can only get hold of something that smells like a horse!' The flowers of the lime seem particularly strong at night, but are also sweet during the day.

SCENTS TO STIR MEMORIES
The final appeal may be, as with Miss Jekyll and the primrose wood, the stirring up of memories. She mentions especially her travels in the islands of the Greek archipelago, recalled 'in a way far more distinct than can be done by a mere mental effort of recollection' by the scents of shrubs in her garden, 'many of them at home in dry and rocky places in far-away lower latitudes . . .' (*Wood and Garden*).

To have a well-remembered garden it seems that some sweet-smelling plant will do more than paved terraces, colourful borders or ornamental pools. 'The sense of smell has also its peculiar province, a strange power of conjuring up the past, being bound up with memory because at some early stage of racial development it has been, like the sense of taste, necessary for the protection of life, and we shall therefore carry away a lasting recollection of the garden, if . . . the air is heavy with scent of some particular flower, or succession of flowers . . .' (Sir George Sitwell, *On the Making of Gardens*).

Most of Miss Jekyll's favourite flowers have a scent, and among roses she especially mentions Madame Alfred Carriére and Blairrii No. 2. But regarding favourite foliage plants she writes often of bergenia and grey-leaved ones such as *Senecio laxifolius* or the Helichrysums. She devotes a page to describing the beauty of the leaves of lady's mantle (*Alchemilla*) and a special favourite amongst flowering shrubs is the *Kalmia*. She writes: 'It seems a loss when a flower has no smell, like the lovely *Kalmia*. This beautiful bush was one of the treasures of the old home shrub-garden' (*Children and Gardens*).

Permanent memorials

A PORTRAIT

William Nicholson had been a personal friend of Ned Lutyens for many years, and since the war he had also been a neighbour in Apple Tree Yard, the mews cottage of 7 St James's Square where Lutyens had the Delhi office. It was through Lutyens that Gertrude Jekyll was eventually persuaded to sit for William Nicholson, which was an achievement in itself. She was at first not only reluctant but horrified at the idea, saying that she was not a paintable kind of person and she could not spare the time. The persuasive charm of her old friend and the adaptability of the artist won the day and throughout most of October and November of 1920 the rather unofficial 'sittings' took place. In most of them the painter was condemned to work in lamp light, as she insisted on working during the best hours of the day. In the intervals Nicholson turned his attention to an old pair of gardening boots, gratefully using for them the valuable daylight which she refused to waste on herself.

The portrait was exhibited at the Grafton Gallery in the spring of 1921 and now hangs in the National Portrait Gallery. The portrait is important as a work of art but also on account of its picture of Miss Jekyll's character. The artist wrote that he hoped he had put 'a little of her serene charm' into the painting. But the portrait of the boots has in some ways become almost more significant. Miss Jekyll's boots have acquired over the years the position of a kind of symbol in the gardening world.

Gertrude Jekyll has been described both as gentle and fierce. She could be either. She had little patience with indifference or stupidity and could settle both with quiet but devastating remarks. She was deeply, but unfussily, religious and at the same time she had a keen sence of fun and delight in adventure with children, understanding their love of magic and make-believe.

If all this is linked together there emerges a composite picture which has been clearly caught by William Nicholson. In spite of all the hard work accomplished and her respect for the good use of time she still gave a feeling of serenity. She sits in her chair, a stout, round figure, dressed in her usual style of voluminous blue serge.

THE LAST SUMMER

During her last summer, 1932, she was only able to see her plants from the wheel-chair which Lutyens had given to her, and she was apologising to a friend in a letter dated 26th August for not having written earlier in reply: 'The delay is because of my infirmities — my years are eighty-eight and there are times when my doctor keeps me very close on account of a worn-out heart, so that many things that I ought to do have to be set aside.' She died on 8th December after a short illness, having celebrated her eighty-ninth birthday on the 29th November.

Miss Jekyll has been described as the first horticultural Impressionist, translating gardening into terms of painting. But she was not only a gardener in colour — she understood as an artist the use of light and shade.

In 1934 her memorial, designed by Sir Edwin Lutyens, was erected in Busbridge churchyard. The inscription reads: 'Artist, Gardener, Craftswoman'. The order is significant as it implies that the second and third qualifications depend on the first. More important is her permanent memorial in the ideas and designs which she has passed on to all future generations.

GERTRUDE JEKYLL'S GARDENS TODAY

It is difficult to keep a garden as it has been kept by someone else; however much one tries to copy ideas small personal differences will creep in which give an individual character.

Miss Jekyll's own garden at Munstead Wood is well cared for now; it has many of the same features and the grass paths still lead through the woodland. The garden at Millmead is kept well; the small summerhouse built by Lutyens is well established now and has an air of antiquity about it.

Some other gardens, quite different in size and type, are still much as they were originally designed but again there are alterations through

William Nicholson's painting of Miss Jekyll's gardening boots was accomplished during the intervals between her sittings for her portrait.

change of ownership. One of these is 100 Cheyne Walk, in London, originally belonging to Sir Hugh Lane. The house is now converted into flats, but the main structure of the Lutyens garden is the same. An interesting changeover is that of Nashdom, near Taplow, Buckinghamshire, built by Lutyens for Prince Alex Dolgorouki as a fabulous villa for weekend river parties. It is now Nashdom Abbey, the home of twenty-seven Benedictine monks.

There are a number of gardens showing her influence or illustrating her ideas either intentionally or quite independently. In some of these examples her influence has been direct, in others there are ideas of which she would have approved. For instance, there is a suggestion of hers which is illustrated at the Waterperry Horticultural Centre,

Wheatley, Oxford: 'The michaelmas daisies are so important in September and October that it is well worth while to give them a separate place, in addition to their use with other flowers in the mixed border.'

In the Savill Gardens, Windsor, there are instances of her suggestions of sending a climbing rose or clematis up into an old fruit-tree or a holly. Some of these are also to be seen in the gardens of Sissinghurst Castle, Kent.

At Folly Farm, Sulhamstead, Berkshire, there are borders of her much loved grey plants — sprawling shrubs of lavender, senecio, iris foliage, and a fine clump of acanthus. The present owners are keen to preserve the original Lutyens-Jekyll design and have been assisted in this by Mr Lanning Roper. Obviously, owing to present labour conditions the garden plan, conceived when labour was not a problem, now has to be simplified. 'So good', writes Mr Lanning Roper, 'is the original design and the basic planting of hedges and trees, that it has not suffered from simplification.'

At Wisley, Surrey, there are groups of lilies between the rhododendrons — Miss Jekyll mentions several visits to the Wisley garden (in *Wood and Garden*), when it belonged to Mr G. F. Wilson.

At Bodnant, Talycafn, Gwynedd, there are slabs of stone used as a border paving between the grass and the edge of the flower-beds. At Great Dixter, East Sussex, there is a strong Jekyll feeling about the garden, giving ample evidence of Mrs Nathaniel Lloyd's appreciation of her ideas, continued by Mr Christopher Lloyd: grey-leafed plants, lavender, mulleins, etc. Clumps of meconopsis flourish at Great Dixter, the credit for which Mrs Lloyd gave to Miss Jekyll.

One of the most exciting restorations of a Jekyll-Lutyens garden is going on today in Somerset. Hestercombe House stands at the foot of the south-facing slope of the Quantocks, overlooking Taunton Deane. (It is at present owned by the Crown Commissioners and has been leased by the Somerset County Council since 1953 as the headquarters of the County's Fire Service.) Of the original design Christopher Hussey wrote: 'The Hestercombe gardens represent the peak of the collaboration with Miss Jekyll and his (Lutyens's) first application of her genius to classical garden design on a grand scale.'

Under the combined direction of the Chief Fire Officer and the County Architect, extensive investigation into the possible restoration of these historic gardens, using the original plans, was begun in 1970 — copies of some of the plans being kindly lent by the Department of Landscape Architecture, University of California, Berkeley. The gardening was worked out to take place in phases over a period of about five years, and it is hoped that the actual replanting, started in 1972, may be completed by 1977. Research for the replanting was carried out by the Somerset County Architect's Department, and although the gardens are being furnished exactly according to the original plans, it has been found necessary in certain cases to substitute perennials where annuals were indicated before.

In the meantime, the Fire Brigade are most co-operative in allowing visitors to the house and garden, but they ask that as far as possible organised parties should be taken and permission obtained by application beforehand by telephoning Taunton 87222. Eventually it is hoped to open the house and garden officially to the public on certain days in the year.

The stonework is being restored by the Crown Estate Office and this, with much of the planting, is now well under way.

THE PRINCIPAL EVENTS OF GERTRUDE JEKYLL'S LIFE

1843 Gertrude Jekyll born
1848 Move to Bramley House
1854 Crimean War (to 1856)
1861 Enrolls as a pupil at Kensington School of Art
1863 Visits the Near East with the Newtons
1866 Death of Mary Newton. Visit to Paris
1868 Visit to Italy
1869 Move to Wargrave
1875 Gives advice on the interior of Eaton Hall
1876 Death of father. Move to Munstead Heath
1881 Asked to judge at the Botanic Show
1889 First meeting with Edwin Lutyens
1891 Consults eye specialist. Death of Barbara Bodichon
1894 Moves into 'the hut'
1895 Death of mother
1897 Receives the Victoria Medal of Honour from Royal Horticultural Society. Moves into Munstead Wood
1899 *Wood and Garden*
1900 *Home and Garden*
1901 *Lilies for English Gardens* and *Wall and Water Gardens*
1902 *Roses for English Gardens*
1904 *Old West Surrey*
1906 Death of H. B. Brabazon
1907 *Flower Decoration in the House*
1908 *Colour in the Flower Garden. Children and Gardens*
1910 Work starts on Great Dixter
1912 *Gardens for Small Country Houses*
1918 *Garden Ornament*
1920 William Nicholson paints her portrait and her gardening boots
1925 *Old English Household Life*
1932 Death of Gertrude Jekyll

BIBLIOGRAPHY

Works by Gertrude Jekyll

Wood and Garden; Longmans Green, 1899.
Home and Garden; Longmans Green, 1900.
Lilies for English Gardens; Country Life, 1901.
Wall and Water Gardens; Country Life, 1901.
Roses for English Gardens (with Edward Mawley); Country Life, 1902.
Old West Surrey; Longmans Green, 1904.
Some English Gardens; Longmans Green, 1904.
Flower Decoration in the House; Country Life, 1907.
Colour in the Flower Garden; Country Life, 1908. (3rd edition, 1914, entitled *Colour Schemes for the Flower Garden*).
Children and Gardens; Country Life, 1908.
Gardens for Small Country Houses (with Lawrence Weaver); Country Life, 1912.
Garden Ornament (with Christopher Hussey); Country Life, 1918.
Old English Household Life; B. T. Batsford, 1925.
A Gardener's Testament; Country Life, 1937.

Selected works relating to Gertrude Jekyll

A Blessed Girl; Lady Emily Lutyens; Rupert Hart-Davis, 1953.
Gertrude Jekyll; Francis Jekyll; Jonathan Cape, 1934.
Miss Jekyll; Betty Massingham; Country Life, 1966.
The Life of Sir Edwin Lutyens; Christopher Hussey; Country Life, 1953.

INDEX